CW00696316

The
Prosperity
Handbook

Gems to enrich your life
and pocket.

Compiled by
Shaun de Warren

WELLSPRING PUBLICATIONS LIMITED
46 Cyril Mansions, Prince of Wales Drive
London SW11 4HW, England

THE PROSPERITY HANDBOOK
2nd Printing 1991

Also from Wellspring

By Shaun de Warren

YOU ARE THE KEY – A Guide to Self-Discovery

THE MIRROR OF LIFE – Your Adventure
in Self-Discovery

In collaboration with Susan Mayne and Sue Lake

THE 10-DAY BROWN RICE DIET – A Journey Towards
Inner and Outer Wellbeing

Compilations

THE RELATIONSHIPS HANDBOOK – Jewels to Bring Love
and Happiness

THE HEALTH HANDBOOK – Pearls to Inspire Healing

*For details of Shaun de Warren's other publications, tapes,
lectures, and workshops, please write to:* WELLSPRING

By Chuck Spezzano, Ph.D.

AWAKEN THE GODS – Aphorisms to Remember the Way Home

ISBN 0 9513520 1 6

Printed and bound in Great Britain by
Biddles Ltd, Guildford and King's Lynn

From the one Source
through many...

Acknowledgements

I acknowledge the Source of all for the wisdom in this handbook, though many people have spoken the words.

I also acknowledge Jeanette Hart for her beautiful handwriting; Brian and Susan Mayne, Sue Lake, and Jeanette Hart for their assistance in selecting the quotations and Gill Coupland for design and production.

Prosperity is ours
already
It is the very nature
of our being and seeks
to express itself.

When I enjoy
my money
'it makes 'it easier
to accumulate
more.

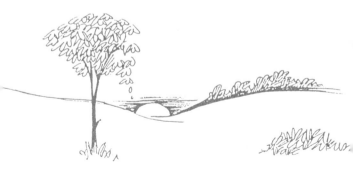

There is no shortage
of supply
There is only a shortage
of demand.

It pays to get definite
about prosperity.
If you want prosperity
to get definite
about you.

You will never
be given anything
until you are ready
to give it to
yourself.

Only you can do it
only you have the power
      to change your life
or any part of it
No-one can or should
         do it for you.

I think prosperous
   and wholesome thoughts
and miracles happen.

You can have
scarcity
or prosperity right now
Choose!

Whatever
you can see
in your vision
you can produce.

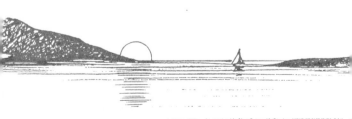

Forgiveness
        and acknowledgement
open the door
        to prosperity.

My consciousness
is the law of
my supply.

I forgive everyone,
    for everything
including myself.

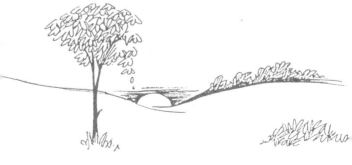

I accept
that what God wants
for me
is my perfect happiness.

You
have to be
fully awake
to make your
dreams come true.

That which I seek
seeks me
for it is who I am
already.

See everything
that happens in your life
as a gift for you
and you are truly
prosperous.

Mediocrity
  is self - inflicted
Genius
  is self - bestowed.

What are you
waiting for ?
Get started !

Live each day
as if it is
the only one you have
It is!

The process of
getting there
is the quality of
being there.

I create a world
in which everyone
is free
to fully express life
and creativity.

Have the courage
to express your creativity
however frightening
that may be.

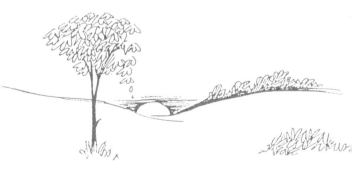

Thank-you
    for the gift of life
and all its riches.

The truth is
everyone
wants to give
and receive
love.

We are not on earth
  to get from one another
but to share the
   spiritual treasures
  that are of God.

Creating money
in my life
is a spiritual activity.

All human wealth
is created
by the mind.

This is not
a rehearsal
This is it!

Imagination
is the
currency of heaven.

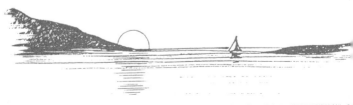

You can have
what you want
or
your reasons for
not having it.

My power
is measured by
the extent to which
I know my relationship
with the universe.

It takes as much
imagination
to create debt as
to create income.

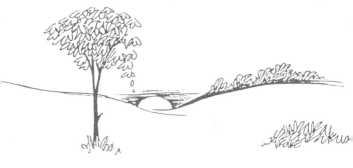

Whatsoever things
ye desire when ye pray,
believe that ye receive them
and ye shall have them.

To get what you
truly want,
don't try and change
the world
Change yourself.

I free myself
from the burden of
blaming others
and take full responsibility
for creating the life
I want.

I love myself
enough
to know I deserve
the best.

Money
is Love
in action.

No-one can give you
the world.
It is already yours
and it is a gift.

To the personality
abundance
is a measure of
quantity;
to soul
it is a measure of
quality.

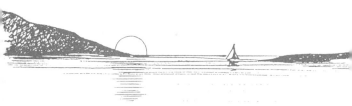

No-one is
truly prosperous
until
everyone is.

Manifestation
is
ninety-eight per cent
inner preparation and
two per cent action.

Prayer at its highest
is gratitude
for that which already is.

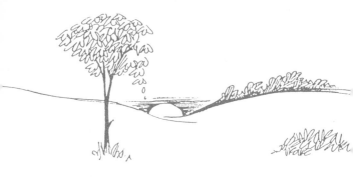

Your best friend,
the wisest person you know
and best counsellor
is yourself.

Open doors
for another
and doors are opened
for you.

Good ideas
don't need money
to get started.

Do unto others
what you would have
others do
unto you.

The strongest single factor
in prosperity consciousness
is self-esteem.

Only what I do
from love
is valuable.

Prosperity consciousness
is knowing I am worth
far more than anyone
can ever pay me.

Let go the burden
of the past and future
and live creatively
in the present

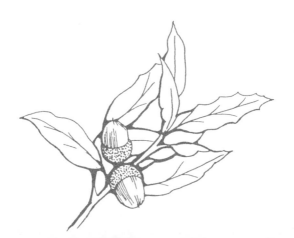

It is the Father's
good pleasure
to give you the Kingdom
and it is your
good pleasure
to receive it.

Do what you believe in
Believe in what you do
All else is a waste of time.

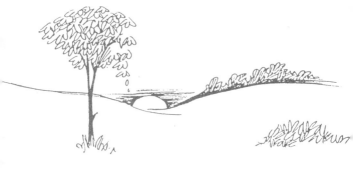

It is as simple as this.
Thinking poor keeps us poor
Thinking rich makes us rich.

Spare
and you have enough
for one

Share
and you have enough
for the multitudes.

Money is not
sacred
It is a toy to play with.

I love money,
money loves me
I'm on the road
to prosperity.

I'm good
I'm expensive
and I'm worth it.

Be ye transformed
by the renewing
of your mind.

Use your dreams
to produce
creative ideas.

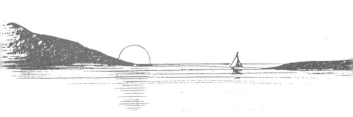

Loafing
is one of the most creative,
money producing things
you can do.

Prosperity
is not an amount
of money
It is a state of
Being.

Creating money
in my life
is a spiritual activity.

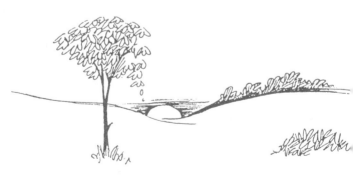

Be a go-giver
rather than
a go-getter.

I can afford to do
anything
I decide I want to do.

Where
there is no vision .
the people perish.

Lack of money
is the root of all
evil.

My thoughts
and desires
are the crop I reap.

Without commitment
nothing
really works.

Make your life exciting
for everyone
to enjoy.

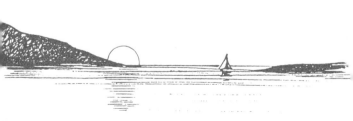

All real work
is love
made visible.

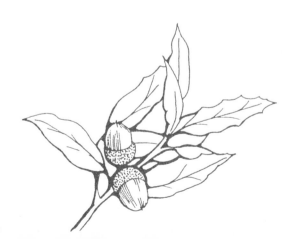

The more I spend
with love
the more I receive.

Trust me
I tell you
you are divine.

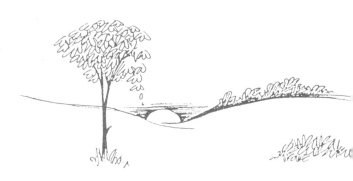

Poor people save;
Rich people bank.

See problems as
opportunities to
discover our treasures.

Overcome fear
and you need overcome
nothing else.

Be still
and know that
I AM
God.

Ask
for what
you want.

It

Already

Is.